Quit Smoking

An Exhaustive Manual Providing Advice And Tactics: Embarking On A Journey Towards A Life Free From Smoking: Verified And Validated Practical Suggestions

(Strategy To Effectively And Definitively Cease Smoking)

Francesco Watt

TABLE OF CONTENT

Examining Your Smoke Behavior 1
Why Is It So Difficult To Give Up? 24
Take Part In Activities Without Drinking 42
The Real Story Behind The Patch. 52
Improve Your Confidence In Self 60
Developing Your Quit Plan: Methods And Approaches 70
Healthy Suggestions And Counselling 83
Helping A Loved One Or Friend To Stop Smoking 107
What Are The Dangerous Ingredients In Cigarettes And How Can They Affect You? 115

Examining Your Smoke Behavior

Examining your smoking patterns, frequency, triggers, patterns, and the impact it has on your life are all important components in analyzing your smoking habits. You can obtain important insights into your smoking habits and make more educated decisions on how to handle them by participating in this self-analysis process. This is a comprehensive resource to help you assess your smoking habits:

Maintain a Smoking Diary: To track your smoking behaviors, start by keeping a notebook. Note specifics like the amount of cigarettes smoked, the time of day, the place, the circumstances, the triggers, and the feelings. This notebook will be a helpful resource for seeing trends and learning more about your smoking habits.

Quantity and Frequency: Analyse your daily cigarette use and frequency of smoking. Take note of whether the frequency of your smoking has altered over time or whether it changes in response to certain circumstances or occasions. You can use this analysis to determine the degree of your smoking habit and how it affects your general health and well-being.

Psychological and Emotional Aspects: Examine the psychological and emotional factors that contribute to your smoking addictions. Consider your feelings about smoking and the advantages it provides. Smoking is frequently used as a coping method for stress, worry, or other unpleasant feelings. Consider whether smoking makes you feel more at ease, self-assured, or able to momentarily block off uncomfortable emotions. You can use this analysis to find better ways to control your emotions.

Social Influences: Take into account how your smoking habits are influenced by others. Smoking is frequently a social activity, and your smoking behavior may be influenced by peer pressure or the need to fit in. Consider if you smoke more in particular social situations or when you're with pals. By examining how social factors affect your smoking, you can become more self-reliant and resist social pressure.

Health Repercussions: Consider the effects of your smoking habit on your body and health. Examine how smoking affects your health in general; consideration of the possible long-term effects might be a powerful incentive to cut back or stop smoking.

The financial ramifications: Compute the monetary expenses linked to your smoking behavior. Calculate how much you spend each month or year on cigarettes. Think about the financial advantages of stopping smoking, like possible savings or the opportunity to use money for more enjoyable and fulfilling pursuits.

Think Back on Past Quit Attempts: If you've made attempts to stop smoking in the past, consider your past experiences. Examine what succeeded and what failed, the difficulties you encountered, and the tactics that came in handy. You can use the insightful information from this study to guide your future attempts to control or stop smoking.

Recall that examining your smoking behaviors is a personal journey that calls for candor, introspection, and a readiness to face the causes of your actions. You will be better able to make decisions regarding your health and well-being as a result of this analysis, which will provide you with a better understanding of your smoking behaviors.

2: The Dangers of Smoking

Why Are Cigarettes Hazardous?

Cigarettes contain almost 4,000 different chemicals, which may surprise you. More than 250 of these have detrimental effects on human health. The following are some of the dangerous chemicals that cigarettes introduce into your body,

Acrolein is a gas that has long been associated with lung cancer, according to a study. According to the CDC, this chemical in cigarettes may damage the lining of your lungs, protecting you from lung disease, and may also impede DNA repair.

1, 3-Butadine is a chemical substance that is utilized in the rubber sector. The CDC states that this element may increase the risk of cancer in the stomach, blood, and lymphatic system.

One chemical that is frequently used to preserve wood is arsenic. It is connected to human cases of cardiac disease. It is also a carcinogen.

Benzene: Other compounds are manufactured using benzene as a raw ingredient. It has been connected to human cases of cancer, most especially leukemia.

One metal that is utilized in the production of batteries is cadmium. This material may prevent the body's DNA from being repaired when it becomes damaged.

One of the most well-known poisons found in cigarettes is probably tar. It's a solid that can be inhaled and increases the risk of cancer. Additionally, tar has been shown by medical researchers to leave a dark, sticky film on your fingernails, teeth, and lungs.

Nicotine and carbon monoxide are two of the hazardous ingredients in cigarettes. As a result of smoking cigarettes, carbon monoxide gas is extremely dangerous to breathe in. This gas is transfused into the bloodstream after entering your lungs, where it actively lowers the amounts of oxygen carried by red blood cells. Increased cholesterol deposits on the inner linings of artery walls have also been linked to carbon monoxide. This may ultimately lead to heart and artery problems.

Cigarettes contain nicotine, a dangerous and highly addictive chemical. Nicotine has been shown to cause artery narrowing, elevated blood pressure, blood flow, and heart rate. Deposits of nicotine can remain in your body for up to eight hours, depending on how often you smoke.

Secondhand smoke: The effects of smokers' activities extend beyond just the smokers themselves. Secondhand smoke from cigarettes can also harm children who are nearby or innocent bystanders. Studies show that exposure to ambient tobacco causes around 46,000 heart disease cases and 3400 deaths from lung cancer. This implies that there is a serious risk to one's health for those who are exposed to this type of smoke at work or at home.

It appears that smoking a cigarette and puffing on it is similar to opening a Pandora's Box based on what it contains. Before we look at how to finally break this habit, let's examine the effects of cigarette smoke on your health and appearance.

What are the health effects of smoking?

Autoimmune Disease: Your body uses the immune system to protect itself against the numerous infections and illnesses that attempt to harm it on a daily basis. Smoking has several common side effects, one of which is that it weakens your immune system, leaving you vulnerable to a variety of respiratory illnesses.

Researchers have also determined that smoking contributes to a number of autoimmune diseases, such as Crohn's disease and rheumatoid arthritis, according to studies. In recent times, scientists studying medicine have discovered data suggesting that smoking increases the risk of adult-onset diabetes (type 2) by as much as 40% among smokers compared to nonsmokers.

Bones: Medical research indicates that smoking reduces bone density directly. Early-starting smokers have an increased risk of developing osteoporosis. Furthermore, it has been shown that smoking reduces estrogen levels in the body, which may cause menopause to start earlier.

Circulatory system: Tobacco smoke includes toxic compounds that damage blood cells and have a negative impact on heart function. Such harm could consist of:

atherosclerosis

Aneurysms

Heart illness, heart attacks, chest pain connected to the heart, high blood pressure, and coronary heart disease

(CHD) are examples of cardiovascular disorders.

Diseases of the peripheral arteries (PAD)

a stroke

which further raises your risk of high blood pressure and heart attacks.

Tobacco use has numerous detrimental impacts on the respiratory system, including:

Inflammation of the trachea, or voice box, reduces lung function and causes "breathlessness" by constricting the airways in the lungs and accumulating mucus in the tubes of the lungs.

Damages the lung's ability to remove pollutants from the air, which can cause a buildup of toxic compounds and lung damage.

increases the risk of lung infections, wheezing, and coughing could result in long-term harm to the lung's air sacs

How can smoking affect one's appearance?

It's true that smoking ruins your appearance. This is precisely how:

Under-eye bags: don't you perspire when you can't sleep well, and your face will look like a map with holes in it?

An autoimmune skin condition related to psoriasis may manifest even if you have never touched a cigar. An investigation done in 2007 found that smokers have an increased chance of developing this illness. Your chance of developing psoriasis increases by more than 60% if you smoke a pack of cigarettes a day for the next ten years or less while you are between the ages of eleven and twenty. Over this age range, the likelihood of developing psoriasis increases even further.

It is a well-known fact that teeth can become stained by nicotine derived from cigarettes.

Prolonged cigarette smoking can cause premature aging, which is characterized by early wrinkles and may actually make you appear older than you are. It's true that smoking hastens aging. This can be explained by the fact that The skin dries up and ages more quickly when it doesn't get enough of the nutrients it needs.

Smoking and Skin Health

Would you smoke if the negative effects of smoking were evident on your face every time you glanced in the mirror?

Would you still smoke if you could see wrinkles, fine lines, and red capillaries forming on your face after each cigarette you smoked?

Maybe no one would if the indications were readily apparent. Maybe fewer people would smoke up or purchase another packet. The effects on the skin are cumulative and long-lasting, even though the benefits are not noticeable right away.

The greatest organ in your body is your skin, and smoking cigarettes harms it. A few negative consequences of smoking on your skin are listed below.

Low Oxygen Delivery from Blood Vessels: Impaired Skin Health

Smoking thins blood vessels, which limits the amount of blood that can pass through them. The blood's levels of oxygen and nutrients are also decreased. These elements have a major effect on skin health.

The body of a smoker experiences lower blood oxygen levels and impaired circulation. The epidermis and the rest of the body's cells depend on oxygen and other blood-borne nutrients to remain healthy.

This is brought on by inadequate blood flow and a deficiency of oxygen, which is necessary for skin repair.

The skin tone could seem grayer or paler. The development of facial wrinkles and other early indicators of aging skin makes poor skin health evident. A smoker's mouth will have wrinkles or "cigarette lines," which are brought on by their continual lip pursing.

Wrinkles and Indications of Early Ageing

Cigarette smoking is another major element that contributes to skin aging, even though excessive sun exposure is one of the main causes. Studies show that smoking accelerates the aging process of the skin compared to exposure to sunshine.

The appearance of wrinkles is one indicator of aging skin. Damage to collagen and elastin, two components of skin, leads to wrinkles.

Extensive research indicates that heavy smokers are more likely to get wrinkles than occasional or never smokers.

In a highly interesting study, participants were asked to determine the age of smokers and nonsmokers based only on the images of the people. According to the findings, nonsmokers were frequently perceived as being younger than their true age, whereas smokers were typically perceived as being older.

Techniques for formulating objectives and making a strategy

Making a strategy and establishing goals can be very effective strategies for kicking an addiction. The following techniques can help you create objectives and draft a plan:

Establish SMART objectives: SMART stands for precise, measurable, realistic, applicable, and time-bound objectives. This means that your goals ought to be specific, measurable, reasonable, pertinent to your driving forces, and have an end date.

Dissect Your Objectives: Your motivation will remain high, and you will succeed if you break down your bigger ambitions into smaller, more achievable tasks. Establish a schedule for finishing each of the tasks that must be taken in order to achieve your bigger objectives.

Seek Expert Assistance: To develop a customized strategy for kicking an addiction, think about getting assistance from an expert, like a therapist or addiction specialist. They can offer continuous support, assist in identifying your triggers, and help you create coping techniques.

Locate Assistance: Seek out support groups or a friend or relative who can help you on your path to recovery from addiction. Talking to someone while you're having difficulties can really help.

Give Yourself a Treat: Enjoy the victories you have along the path. Incentives can boost your motivation and add enjoyment to the task at hand. Choose constructive methods to indulge yourself, such as seeing a movie, indulging in a favorite meal, or spending time doing something you enjoy.

Recall that recovering from addiction is a process, and reaching your objectives may need patience and perseverance. If you make a mistake, don't quit and remember to enjoy every little accomplishment as you go.

.

Getting Assistance

Getting help is essential to beating addiction and staying in recovery. The following are some methods for locating assistance:

Support Teams: Think about becoming a member of a support group like Narcotics Anonymous (NA) or Alcoholics Anonymous (AA). These support groups offer a helpful network of people who are pursuing recovery as well.

Therapy: You might want to think about getting assistance from a therapist or addiction specialist who can offer you personalized support and direction on your road to recovery.

Friends and Family: Never undervalue the influence of your loved ones' support. Make contact with your helpful and supportive family and friends.

Online Support: For individuals in recovery, including forums and online support groups.

Self-Helding: While you're healing, look after yourself. This can entail engaging in physical activity, practicing meditation, or making time for hobbies.

Sober Living: For individuals in recovery, sober living houses offer a secure and encouraging environment.

Peer assistance: Programmes that offer peer assistance, including peer mentorship or recovery coaches, can offer advice and support from people who have gone through comparable experiences.

Keep in mind that each person's road to recovery is different, and what works for one may not work for another. It's critical to investigate several forms of support and determine which ones are most effective for you. Never hesitate to ask for assistance and support when you need it.

The value of assistance in kicking an addiction

Getting support is essential to kicking an addiction and staying in recovery. Here are some explanations for why assistance is crucial:

Responsibility: Having a support network can encourage you to stay on course and hold you responsible for your choices.

Understanding: Getting support from those who have gone through comparable circumstances can help one feel understood and validated, which is beneficial for the healing process.

Emotional Support: Recovering from addiction can be a stressful process, and you may find it easier to handle the difficulties and pressures of recovery if you have emotional support.

Help with childcare or transport is an example of practical support that can make the healing process less taxing and easier.

Motivation: When things get difficult, having the support of others helps keep you going on the road to recovery.

The process of recovering requires patience and hard work. The path might be more successful and easier if you have a support system. Never hesitate to ask for assistance and support when you need it.

Why Is It So Difficult To Give Up?

According to the study, quitting smoking takes around thirty tries to be successful. And only one of them truly offers salvation.

It can be quite difficult to stop smoking, whether you smoke once a day or once a week. Whichever you are, there is no simple way to stop because it is a physical addiction as well as a psychological habit.

In actuality, nicotine is one of the main components used in the manufacturing of tobacco. Nicotine gives you a short-term high and is a highly addictive drug.

Regular nicotine intake acclimates your body to the drug's "highness" and "feel good" effects on the brain, which makes you crave it after you quit smoking. When you're trying to quit smoking, your cravings may get so strong that you can't resist them.

Smoking is typically used as a coping mechanism for anxiety, boredom, and despair. Some people smoke as a fast method to decompress, release tension, and get new perspectives on life.

There are instances when smoking may be the result of peer pressure. Observing your friends or coworkers smoke makes you feel as though you should share something in order to get along with them. It might also be your default reaction at the end of an extremely demanding day or while you're taking a break from work.

Whatever your motivation, you can effectively stop smoking. By successfully stopping, we mean that you will discover a healthier substitute for smoking. The secret would be to examine and correct the routines and habits that have become ingrained with the addiction.

Even though you've failed numerous times, we can guarantee you that there's a very good chance you won't smoke this time.

Fortunately, you may permanently kick the habit of smoking with the help of this advice.

Two: Identifying Addiction's Patterns and Triggers

Understanding and controlling addictive behaviors requires an awareness of addiction patterns and triggers. Although there are many different types of addiction (such as substance abuse, gambling, gaming, etc.), the underlying patterns and triggers are usually the same. Here are a few crucial things to think about:

Patterns of behavior: Patterns are what addictive behaviors usually follow. Increasing concern about the substance or behavior, a lack of control over usage, continuing to participate despite negative effects, and difficulties cutting back or stopping are a few examples of these. It can be easier to identify addiction when these patterns are recognized.

Environmental triggers: Specific environments or situations have the potential to spark off addictive behavior. These triggers could include being among people who support or engage in similar habits, being in environments connected to substance misuse, or experiencing stressful situations that make someone turn to an addictive substance or behavior for solace.

Emotional triggers: It's possible that emotions play a role in the emergence of addiction. Some people turn to drugs or other unhealthy habits as a coping mechanism for negative emotions such as loneliness, stress, anxiety, or despair. Knowing the connection between specific emotions and addictive conduct might help in identifying triggers.

Environmental triggers: Specific environments or situations have the potential to spark off addictive behavior. These triggers could include being among people who support or engage in similar habits, being in environments connected to substance misuse, or experiencing stressful situations that make someone turn to an addictive substance or behavior for solace.

Emotional triggers: It's possible that emotions play a role in the emergence of addiction. Some people turn to drugs or other unhealthy habits as a coping mechanism for negative emotions such as loneliness, stress, anxiety, or despair. Knowing the connection between specific emotions and addictive conduct might help in identifying triggers. Environmental triggers: Specific environments or situations have the potential to spark off addictive behavior. These triggers could include being among people who support or engage in similar habits, being in environments connected to substance misuse, or experiencing stressful situations that make someone turn to an addictive substance or behavior for solace.

Emotional triggers: It's possible that emotions play a role in the emergence of addiction. Some people turn to drugs or other unhealthy habits as a coping mechanism for negative emotions such as loneliness, stress, anxiety, or despair. Knowing the connection between specific emotions and addictive behavior might help in identifying triggers.

Understanding Addiction's Physiological Aspects

Addiction is a complex issue, having both psychological and physiological aspects. It is typified by an obsessive need to use drugs or indulge in a certain habit, even when doing so could have a negative impact on one's general well-being, relationships, and health. Let's examine the physiological and psychological components of addiction in more detail:

a. Neurochemical alterations: The brain's reward system, which includes the release of neurotransmitters like dopamine, is often altered by addiction. By creating a feeling of reward and strengthening the addictive habit, these drugs aid in the reinforcement of pleasurable activities.

b. Tolerance and withdrawal: withdrawal symptoms may appear, which are the body's attempt to acclimatize to life without the substance.

c. Neuroadaptation: Abuse of substances can cause the brain to change how it functions to compensate for the presence of the substance. Decision-making, impulse control, and other cognitive functions may change as a result of modifications to the structure and function of the brain.

d. Craving and relapse: Even after a period of sobriety, it might be difficult to resist the inclination to relapse due to physiological changes in the brain that generate intense wants for the addictive substance.

Addiction's psychological aspects

Reinforcement and conditioning: Addiction involves the reinforcement of conduct due to the rewarding benefits of the substance or behavior. Repetitive positive reinforcement can lead to the development of conditioned responses, in which cues associated with substance use elicit cravings and the desire to participate in the addictive behavior.

a. Coping mechanism: Addiction is a coping mechanism that some people use to deal with psychological issues, trauma, distress, and stressful situations. These feelings may be momentarily subdued by the addictive habit or drug, making people dependent on it to regulate their emotional health.

c. Co-occurring mental health issues: Addiction and mental health disorders that commonly co-occur include depression, anxiety, and post-traumatic stress disorder (PTSD). These problems could encourage the development and upkeep of addiction,

d. Environmental variables: Social, cultural, and environmental factors can have an impact on the development of addiction. The accessibility of drugs, social pressure, and cultural norms can all have an impact on a person's propensity to become addicted.

Why Do Other Methods of Smoking Cessation Not Work?

Actually, they do function. At least some of them.On occasion.Additionally, for certain individuals. However, they have drawbacks that make them more likely to fail in the long run and could be the reason you are still sacrificing a significant portion of your life to be able to smoke.

Shall we examine a couple more approaches? To ascertain potential trouble spots or areas where they may have already caused you trouble

Changing abruptly

Giving up abruptly is known as going cold turkey. You may smoke three packs of cigarettes a day or twelve smokes over a cup of coffee, one instant, and then not smoke at all. Not one cigarette at all. At all. Indeed, it is an extreme step that is quite taxing on the body and the mind, yet the data seem to indicate that most people choose to do it.

Approximately 80% of persons who have quit smoking reportedly do so using the "cold turkey" method—a term used colloquially to refer to suddenly quitting an addiction—although the exact percentages from different research vary.

Restrictions

When someone wants to stop smoking, they usually start cold turkey. It doesn't seem to work every time, as many people—including the majority of this book's readers—fail at it. The likelihood of failure is actually rather high. This approach doesn't work for most of us because it requires a great deal of work, physical strain, and misery.

Substitute medication for nicotine.

NRT, as specialists and wannabe experts refer to it, is only an alternative method of supplying the body with nicotine without the use of tobacco. Nicotine is available in the following forms: inhalers, gum, patches, and nasal sprays. While NRT is one of the most popular medicinal techniques for quitting smoking (another phrase specialists like to use), it is not without drawbacks.

Restrictions

First of all, NRT is not a cure for nicotine addiction. Secondly, obtaining nicotine into the body still requires a significant amount of time, money, and effort. Thirdly, adverse outcomes might occur.

Grave ones. Individuals who already have heart problems may be more susceptible to severe illness, and skin irritation and allergies are constant risks.

Additional drugs

Have you heard of drugs like bupropion, nortriptyline, clonidine, varenicline, etc.? Most likely not. All of these drugs, which are available in different forms, have been shown to be successful in helping people quit smoking.

Restrictions

Similar to other medications, they may also cause a number of unpleasant side effects. A few of the many potential drawbacks include nausea, vomiting, anxiety, dizziness, fever, irregular heartbeat, headache, depression, exhaustion, dry mouth, constipation, flatulence, nausea, vomiting, anxiety, and stomach pain. Furthermore, there's always that uncomfortable feeling of being drug dependent.

Alternative replacements

These days, electronic cigarettes are the most often used substitutes. They are available in many forms, but they all contain a unique vapor that mimics tobacco smoke but is less damaging to the lungs. It is also expected to be far less expensive overall than standard smokes.

Restrictions

Although they seem fantastic, there is still a lot we don't know about electronic cigarettes. It will take time and more research to determine whether using electronic cigarettes is indeed a safer option than smoking tobacco cigarettes, as the so-called e-liquids contain a number of potentially dangerous ingredients. Some people have already asserted that smoking electronic cigarettes could be even riskier than traditional tobacco use.

The fact that switching from one addiction to another is probably not the wisest course of action could be another problem. How do you feel?

Cognitive behavioral intervention

The field of psychotherapy is very familiar with cognitive behavioral therapy. With remarkable success, it is used to treat (or lessen) anxiety, depression, and a host of other mental illnesses. Indeed, smoking is included in the list.

Restrictions

It's a type of psychotherapy that immediately entails a significant investment of time, money, and potential social shame. Even after all that effort, cognitive behavioral therapy—like the majority of smoking cessation techniques—is still far from ideal, and as a result, it frequently fails or only lasts temporarily.

The use of acupuncture

We are conversing now, huh? For those of us in the West, acupuncture represents an alternate method of treating a variety of health-related problems, including pain, depression, obesity, and allergies. Since it can also be used to treat addiction, a lot of smokers choose to give it a shot.

Restrictions

Ignoring the obvious—letting someone inject your body with numerous needles—there are a number of additional drawbacks. There are certain possibilities of (unintentional) injuries and infections, although side effects are rare (as long as the acupuncturist is a true professional in the field). But maybe the largest issue with acupuncture is that it frequently just doesn't work for smokers.

The use of hypnosis

Another method is using hypnosis to overcome a person's addiction to smoking. Though most of us find it highly mysterious, hypnosis is actually a relatively common type of psychotherapy. The basic tenet is that because our minds are far more receptive to behavioral changes during hypnosis, quitting some bad habits—like smoking, for example—should be considerably simpler at this time.

Restrictions

Once more, hypnotherapy frequently has very little to no effect on smokers. It requires money, time, and effort in addition to having that unsettling "what are they doing to me?" feeling.

Take Part In Activities Without Drinking

Everywhere we look, there is a pre-event cocktail hour taking place, or someone is texting us asking if we'd like to get together for a few drinks. These kinds of things can be intellectually, financially, and physically taxing. We tend to reach for a shot of scotch or a glass of wine out of habit so frequently that we eventually find ourselves "pouring one" without giving it any thought.

Therefore, it's important to remember that "conscious consumption" refers to much more than just purchasing. It also demands that we understand just how drinking alcohol impacts our bodies, thoughts, and the environment. We must learn to be more intentional about when and how we drink or don't drink if we want to improve our connection with ourselves.

Regardless of your past or present drinking patterns, it's critical to challenge yourself to step outside of your routine "comfort zones" and occasionally give your body a rest.

Whether you can't remember the last time you spent a weekend without drinking or you've been sober for months but still feel the need to indulge occasionally, these are really useful techniques you may use to connect and communicate without drinking:

Engage in non-alcoholic pursuits.

People should be doing something far more active and exciting with the time they spend outside of bars and clubs. The next time you plan a get-together with your friends, make sure to include some non-alcoholic options.

You may play pick-up sports, go for a walk or a bike ride, watch a play or movie, or go to an art opening or music concert. Choose an activity that doesn't promote drinking or a place that doesn't sell beer or other alcoholic beverages. By doing this, you will be able to reduce your alcohol intake, increase your energy, and become more active, all of which will contribute to your general health.

You might also cook or bake something unusual or elegant. Try preparing something that requires the attention and ability of two experienced hands, such as pastries or sweets.

Bread is an excellent alternative if you're searching for something to occupy your hands without having to focus all of your attention on it. You also get to enjoy eating it after baking.

Prepare a dinner or make some stock.

If you're the practical type, get ready for the upcoming week by chopping veggies, soaking your dry beans, or making prepared freezer dinners.

It's not fancy by any means, but it will be fun to turn on your favorite show, podcast, or record and invite your closest friends and family to join you. In addition to being tremendously enjoyable to make when you have a few extra hours, stocks can potentially cut down on food waste.

Alternatively, you may curl up with a complete spread of snacks and enjoy a movie or sporting event. Yes, you could indulge in Oreos and Doritos, but choosing festive, healthful options like vegan cheese boards and cauliflower wings is much more enjoyable.

Visit the library to choose a fresh book to read.

If the local branches close in the evening, head to the café with a book you've been meaning to read. If there are any in your area that let it, you could even set up a tent in the bookstore.

Take an after-hours yoga class.

You will wake up the next day feeling fantastic—much more amazing than you could have felt after downing several beers the night before—but yoga will hurt.

You could do a tonne of things that don't include drinking booze. You'll have plenty of options if you're a little inventive. You will eventually come to appreciate them more than the ones that include a lot of drinks.

You must do what the following Step discusses in order to make this Step a reality: hang out with people who don't drink.

2: Getting Ready

You need to get ready once you've determined whether you're ready to give up smoking and have made the decision to follow through. There will be a few different things involved in this portion of the journey, but the most important thing is to make sure you know what to do and what to anticipate.

Make Research

It's usually a good idea to research whatever you are bringing into your life for the first time. As I've said before, it guarantees that you are aware of what to anticipate. When conducting research, you may look at things like symptoms to anticipate, know-how advice, or even things your friends and family can do to support you as you tackle the difficult work ahead of you.

Additionally, you should make sure you research strategies for managing the symptoms you are about to encounter. Managing mental health issues such as sadness and stress can be challenging, particularly if you are not able to smoke, which has likely been your go-to coping strategy for years. You may occasionally require medical assistance (see four).

Choose a Start Date.

Many individuals promise to quit right away, but as soon as procrastination sets in, they say things like "After tomorrow," and so on. It is a never-ending loop. Choosing the ideal time to quit is mostly up to you and your personal tastes. It's possible that you're going through a difficult moment and aren't feeling motivated right now. That's quite acceptable; you must keep in mind that you are doing this for yourself and that quitting is primarily for your satisfaction, happiness, and health, even though it may have an impact on many individuals in your life.

After you've smoked your last pack of cigarettes, a lot of individuals advise quitting; they just stop buying after that. This is a smart move since it will give you the opportunity to mentally get ready to break a habit that you may have had for a long time. Additionally, you won't consider it to be a waste of a pack of smokes, which, depending on where you live, might be really costly. To others, it appears as though they are free from the temptation of a half-pack of cigarettes that are waiting to be smoked in their drawer. Having that last pack of cigarettes out of your possession will undoubtedly benefit you.

Of course, some individuals decide on a particular date. It can be their child's birthday or the end of the Christmas season when all the parties and celebrations end. It truly depends on you, your tastes, and even the events and celebrations you take part in, as I've mentioned previously.

Choose the Technique You Wish to Try

You can attempt to stop smoking using a variety of strategies. Of course, every technique works differently on different individuals, and it can have a different impact on you than on someone else. These techniques often cover a broad variety of actions you might do to ease the process of quitting. This could entail gradually cutting back on smoking one day at a time or one week at a time. For some people, cutting back on their daily cigarette consumption can be beneficial. For instance, you might start out smoking one pack of cigarettes in a single day, but as you start to wean yourself off, you might find that by the end of the week, there are still a few cigarettes in that pack. Until you feel ready to give up smoking altogether, you can gradually start cutting back on the number of cigarettes you smoke each day.

Of course, there are a lot of alternative approaches besides this one. For instance, you may discover that using an e-cigarette or other type of vapor helps you wean yourself off. There are a lot of things you can do to assist in making the drop go much more smoothly, but you have to figure out which one is best for you—that is, the one that will support you without making you feel worse than you need to be. It could be challenging at first to choose the best approach, but you truly need to know yourself and how you will respond to the change.

The Real Story Behind The Patch.

This is perhaps one of the most well-known quit-smoking products available. They are easy to operate, provide the user discretion, and have a daily, one-time usage.

Some brand names of the patch come with a hefty price tag. If you window shop, you should be able to find something that fits your needs and falls within your desired price range.

There are currently two different types of patches available on the market. The nicotine patch is the first kind. This patch delivers nicotine into the body through a time-release mechanism that eliminates the need for smoking.

You may control the habit and yet get your nicotine fix by doing this. You will start with a powerful patch that contains a significant amount of nicotine when you first start quitting smoking cigarettes.

You will start lowering the amount of nicotine in the patch as you learn to control the habit and no longer feel the need to hold a cigarette in your hand.

The reason this is called a step program is that you will gradually cut back on nicotine until your body no longer craves it as much each day. It is similar to a heroin addict switching from heroin to methadone.

The fact that this method only involves changing out one type of nicotine for another is a drawback.

You are continuing to feed the addiction even if you might not be getting all the other harmful chemicals. Since the addiction isn't being treated, some people might not be able to stop using the patch or gradually reduce the amount of nicotine in it.

The nicotine patch is a more standardized method of quitting cigarettes because it releases nicotine throughout the skin.

In actuality, the patch has been available since 1993 and costs between $20 and $30 per week. It's important to remember that the patch should be kept out of the reach of children and pets, and it's not advised to use it if you are expecting. You should also see your doctor before using the patch if you are breastfeeding or younger than 18 years old.

For best results, the patch should be applied on the upper arm, and your arm should be cleaned and dried before application. After applying the patch, wash your hands, and be sure to dispose of it properly after you take it off.

Frequently, the application site may become itchy or uncomfortable; if this happens, choose another place to utilize it.

You might not want to use the patch if you have sensitive skin.

It could just be an irritant rash if you have a more severe reaction to the patch on your skin, and it becomes excruciating. You might not want to use the patch if you have sensitive skin.

Additional side effects may include headache, drowsiness, dizziness, indigestion, flushing, and moderate nausea during the first few days while your body adjusts to the medicine. You may wish to follow up with your doctor if the symptoms persist.

Call your chemist or doctor at away if you have any of the following symptoms: stress and worry, tremors, an irregular heartbeat, breathing difficulties, or chest pains.

The nicotine patch should only be used temporarily, and although a prescription was once required, it is now available over the counter. Although quitting cigarettes is a wonderful aid, it's not the best solution for quitting.

Medicinal Patch

Herbal patches are an additional type of patch. The time-released herbs in this patch offer the same level of stimulation as nicotine but without the use of actual nicotine. Because the ingredients in this type of medication substitute are all-natural herbs and the patch users are not given nicotine, it is far safer. There is no chance of dependence on these patches because they don't include any substances that are addictive.

This would be a fantastic option for people who are determined to stop smoking but only feel like they need a little help. As these patches may also cause skin irritations, it is imperative that you use them in a private setting the first time you use them.

Because of the patch you are using, you won't have any apparent rashes by doing this.

Patching yourself could be a great way to kick the habit of smoking cigarettes.

Whichever type of patch you choose, make sure you apply it to a part of your body that is not visible and does not have particularly sensitive skin, such as your butt.

You will have a better chance of succeeding because they are time-released, which means you will get your nicotine fix without having to consider smoking one more cigarette.

This will free you up to do other things instead of putting a cigarette in your mouth.

The Tablet

You might also use the anti-smoking medications that are currently available if you are uncomfortable using the patch method. Many of these pills function in the same way as herbal patches and are regarded as herbal substitutes.

To make sure the body thinks it is getting nicotine when it is actually getting an herbal substitute, they offer an alternative to nicotine. As your body begins to receive the nicotine replacement it so desperately needs, you may also want to address the habits that also cause you to smoke.

The body is not getting the actual nicotine from the herbal pill strategy, which implies that these pills could not be effective for everyone. This is one drawback of the approach.

Herbal supplements may cause mild side effects, such as diarrhea, but nothing exceptionally dangerous. This is not a significant factor because smoking cigarettes will do significantly more harm than a loose stool.

Improve Your Confidence In Self

Never question your ability to give up. Try it and see how successful you are!

To effectively stop, you must have self-assurance. According to many experts, smoking is 90% psychologically driven and just 10% physically addictive. Your body will recover from nicotine withdrawals pretty quickly (the worst symptoms normally go away in three days or less), but you may have a much harder time breaking the psychological hold that cigarettes have on you.

You must thus commit to a program that will assist you in quitting smoking and becoming a non-smoker. Working on the mental obstacles preventing you from excelling is perhaps the greatest place to start.

Your success will be mostly determined by two factors:

1. The desire to stop smoking must be present.

2. You have to have confidence in your ability to succeed.

1. Want to kick the habit of smoking

Desire is the foundation of all achievement. Remember this all the time. Just like a small amount of fire produces a small amount of heat, weak desires lead to poor outcomes. - The late Napoleon Hill

Deciding to give up is not the same as desiring to give up. It is entirely up to you to decide whether or not to give off smoking. It's possible that those close to you want you to give up. However, you won't give it your all and will set yourself up for failure if you don't have the drive to give up.

It will be more difficult to quit if you do not feel good about it. This is only one of the many reasons it's imperative to be determined to stop. You'll offer yourself a greater chance of success when you commit.

2. You have to have confidence in your abilities.

"Smoking is not a barrier to stop you; it's just something you have to overcome!"

Unfortunately, a lot of individuals give up before they even begin going. Simply by considering the work at hand, they give up. "Take it one day at a time" and "believe in yourself" are two pieces of advice that many coaches in sports will tell you.

You've already won half the fight if you have confidence in yourself. Recall the times when you demonstrated your strength of will. All you really need to do is get your spirits back up. Find a quit partner who shares your desire to give up smoking so you can support one another.

One may think that life is too short and that there is a lot of work ahead of them. The escape to freedom is frequently doomed before it ever takes off because of this psychological barrier. Taking things one day at a time is the key to avoiding this trap. Every morning, resolve to abstain from nicotine for the duration of the day. Issues and difficulties of the future cannot and should not be transferred into the present.

Your Sources of Motivation

Create a list or, better yet, more understandable notes (like I did). I didn't have a smartphone or any type of personal storage when I started my journey to quit smoking, and it worked out just fine. Don't let this important step slip by using the excuse that you don't have a smartphone.

The following is what you should ask yourself:

What is the main reason I want to stop smoking? If I don't give up my addiction, what will I fear the most?

Write down everything you fear will happen if you continue to smoke, along with your primary motivation for quitting. Use your fear to your advantage if, like me, fear is what drives you to quit, and it's the main reason you're quitting for health reasons.

Here's a sample of what I wrote—be advised it contains some graphic material.

"I need to give up smoking. If I don't quit, I might develop emphysema, COPD, or cancer. I might also end myself hooked up to oxygen and unable to move or breathe. I'll become reliant on others around me and forfeit my independence. For the remainder of my life, my family will have to put up with my constant medical appointments and long-term care needs. I might not feel well for a while. My greatest concern is that I might even require surgery and wake up with a tube put down my neck. Needles, grueling examinations, bed rest, and changing diapers will be my only experiences in life. I might die slowly, gasping for air, and my family might have to go through the agonizing process of determining whether to remove my life support. All of this occurred as a result of my decision to put smoke ahead of my family. My family will always bear the consequences of my selfishness, even after I pass away.

That might sound dramatic, but to me, it's all true. I knew it had to be true because I was hesitant to give up my addiction so much. I had to fear the worst when it came to the effects of smoking.

You are the only one who knows yourself. Whatever it takes to shock you into reality, use that term. Really, you should feel their suffering in addition to reading the words and seeing them in all of their horrible detail.

You may eventually grow insensitive to the notes' ability to inspire you. Knowledge may transform a frightening topic into words that are benign. Writing another note card that is similarly uninviting and/or scary is a simple fix. Write about a new fear, or write about the same one in a different way. Make use of any language that will help you avoid that cigarette for a little while longer.

Here's another letter to myself that takes into account both desire and fear. I wrote, "I want to have a baby but if I continue to smoke, I will be endangering my baby's health," since I knew I couldn't smoke and have children. Because of my smoking, my kid may be extremely underweight, and if the baby needs to be born early for whatever reason, they may suffer from being too light. I will always have to live with the knowledge that I deprived my child of a happy and healthy life. My self-centered obsession could lead the baby to suffer for the remainder of its life or perhaps cause it to pass away. My infant and I could never be around severe chemicals. I'm not able to smoke and be a parent. It is simply not possible. I have to decide between cigarettes and a baby. Is smoking a cigarette really worth the sacrifice I would have to make?

These most intimate messages are meant to serve as a reality check rather than as a form of punishment. Like I did, you might find yourself consulting these notes frequently. If you have smoked for a long time, it could be best to read up on diseases linked to smoking cigarettes and to take very detailed notes.

Make the most of the things that you hold dearest. If you're in love with your appearance right now, consider how smoking will affect your face and how horrible your breath, body, clothes, home, automobile, and everything else you own and travel in will smell, upsetting everyone around you.

You need to be both graphic and genuine. Saying something like, "I'll smell bad," just to be kind to oneself is not enough.

Be truthful and exhaustive.

Remember that these inspirational cards/notes are essential to your success, so don't cut corners because the topic scares you. If you don't quit smoking, you have to be willing to acknowledge your fears and be patient and honest with yourself.

Developing Your Quit Plan: Methods And Approaches

Making the decision to stop smoking is a big step towards getting your health and well-being back. Let's examine the essential elements of developing an effective smoking cessation strategy.

Decide on a Stop Date

Decide on a day to start your path towards quitting smoking. This date needs to be not too far off, giving you time to psychologically be ready without having to make needless delays. Setting a firm date for your quit gives your plan a defined beginning point and fosters a sense of commitment.

Determine What Triggers You

Consider carefully whether circumstances, pursuits, or feelings usually make you want to smoke. Stress, social circumstances, particular locations, or particular routines are examples of common triggers. You may control your desires and prevent relapses by learning about your triggers and creating useful coping mechanisms.

Examine Your Options for Nicotine Replacement Therapy (NRT)

Products for nicotine replacement therapy, like gum, patches, and inhalers, should be taken into consideration. Withdrawal symptoms are lessened with NRT by progressively lowering nicotine dependence. To find out which NRT choices are best for you and how to incorporate them into your quit-smoking strategy, speak with your healthcare physician.

Create Coping Mechanisms

Create an arsenal of coping mechanisms to control cravings and get through difficult circumstances. Engaging in physical activity, mindfulness meditation, deep breathing techniques, or a pastime can all help divert your attention and lessen the temptation to smoke. Try out many methods to find the one that suits you the most.

Change Your Daily Habit

Determine which habits or pursuits were strongly linked to smoking and make the required changes. For example, if you used to smoke during your morning coffee break, think about switching to a healthier habit by having a healthy snack or going for a walk in its place. Overcoming cravings can be made easier by severing the link between particular hobbies and smoking.

Remain upbeat and acknowledge accomplishments.

Stay optimistic as you embark on your road to stop smoking. Celebrate your accomplishments, no matter how tiny, to motivate yourself and recognize your growth. Reward yourself with delicacies or activities related to quitting smoking to reaffirm your commitment and serve as a reminder of the advantages of living a smoke-free life.

Anticipate Withdrawal Symptoms

Be advised that during the quitting process, withdrawal symptoms may manifest. Irritability, restlessness, difficulty focusing, and an increase in hunger are typical symptoms. Remind yourself that these are only transitory symptoms that come with healing. To lessen the discomfort associated with withdrawal, keep wholesome snacks on hand, drink plenty of water, and exercise frequently.

Continue to Strive and Take Advice from Failures

Giving up smoking is a journey that might have obstacles. Please don't be too hard on yourself if you relapse. Rather, take a lesson from it, pinpoint the events or triggers that caused the relapse, and modify your plan as needed. Make the most of failures to strengthen your resolve to succeed and to improve.

Honour Your Achievement

Celebrate your success and recognize the benefits it has brought about for your health and well-being when you successfully reach your goal of quitting smoking. Give yourself a reward that embodies your devotion and perseverance. Make good decisions and stay smoke-free by using this accomplishment as inspiration.

Keep in mind that each person's path is distinct. Therefore, you must modify your strategy to fit your own requirements and situation. Remain steadfast, resilient, and open to the life-changing potential of giving up smoking for a happier, healthier future.

The use of acupuncture

Although there have been stories of acupuncture helping some smokers quit, these claims have not been independently verified and do not have scientific support.

The ancient Chinese treatment of acupuncture involves the insertion of tiny needles into different body areas to treat various ailments. These needles are used to stimulate various locations on the body and ears in order to help people stop smoking. Supporters of the therapy assert that long-lasting benefits result in a decrease in nicotine cravings.

If you want to use this strategy, be careful to do a thorough investigation and keep in mind that there is no real medical study to support the success of this approach—rather, it is purely anecdotal.

Work Out Your Cravings

It is very advantageous to replace tobacco use with regular exercise. It will assist you in managing your cravings as well as helping you keep in shape, as most smokers gain weight when they quit.

Frequent exercise prevents you from gaining too much weight after you stop smoking since, without nicotine, your blood sugar levels will drop, and you'll feel hungry more frequently.

Exercise reduces nicotine cravings: research indicates that focusing on physical activity helps ward off the need to light up a cigarette.

Activity helps to lessen withdrawal symptoms, and this benefit might extend for up to 50 minutes following activity.

Exercise elevates your mood; stopping is linked to depression, and regular exercise might enhance your mental health in general.

Entrance

One technique for inducing an altered state of consciousness in a person is hypnosis. It is utilized as a therapy for pain management and control, and more recently, it has been used to treat other illnesses like obesity. Hypnosis for quitting smoking has received conflicting reviews. Mainly because one in four persons is not able to be hypnotized, making it an ineffective kind of therapy.

A hypnotist tries to explain three main concepts to a smoker who is trying to stop:

Tobacco is toxic and causes bodily harm. Because you depend on your body to survive, you shouldn't abuse it.

Though it may sound absurd when you really think about it, every smoker is aware that they are poisoning themselves, but they tend to put this awareness deep into their subconscious. A hypnotist can instruct a smoker on how to induce self-hypnosis and remind them of this common sense when cravings arise.

To properly ascertain the effectiveness of hypnosis in helping people quit smoking, more investigation is necessary. There are currently few published research, and the available information is unclear.

As you can see, those who are serious about quitting have access to a wide variety of smoking cessation techniques. Your level of devotion will, however, determine whether or not you succeed in your endeavors. Because most of the techniques can reinforce one another, it is advisable to mix them. While nicotine replacement therapy effectively reduces cravings on a physical and psychological level, it is unable to address the feeling that most smokers who are trying to quit experience—that is, not knowing what to do with their mouth and arms—so smokers utilizing this therapy may also want to think about utilizing one or more of these methods.

Electronic Cigarettes

In the e-smoking world, electronic cigarettes—also referred to as vaporizers or mods—are a relatively recent method of quitting smoking.

Although there is still disagreement among researchers on the potential hazards associated with e-cigarettes, most of them concur that they are far less dangerous than traditional cigarettes.

The primary reason given by the majority of e-cigarette users is that they make it easier for them to wean themselves off of traditional tobacco products.

A few justifications for e-cigarettes:

They are a non-combustible way to take nicotine. Most of the poisons included in traditional cigarettes are absent from e-cigarettes. When it comes to handling, they are a simple substitute for traditional cigarettes (most smokers say that not knowing what to do with their hands is a major reason for relapse). E-cigarettes don't harm the environment. Because e-cigarettes only release vaporrather than smoke, they are not dangerous to other people.

Vegetable glycerin and propylene glycol, which are natural byproducts of petroleum and vegetable oil and are allowed by the FDA for use in the food sector, are the main ingredients in e-liquids. Colors, flavorings, and nicotine are additional ingredients. It is noteworthy that an extensive selection of e-liquids is available that have no nicotine at all, making this strategy appropriate for individuals attempting to give up traditional cigarettes completely — without replacing nicotine from cigarettes with any other addictive substance.

According to some research, e-cigarettes and nicotine patches are equally effective methods of quitting smoking, with few side effects. Additionally, compared to nicotine patch users, e-cigarette users are less likely to relapse and resume smoking traditional cigarettes.

To find out if using an e-cigarette increases a user's risk, more research is still required. Thus far, all available research indicates that it is a safe substitute for cigarette smoke.

Healthy Suggestions And Counselling

In addition to harming the smoker, smoking also affects friends, family, coworkers, and other people who breathe in the smoker's tobacco smoke, also known as passed-down cigarette smoke.

Around 300,000 cases of pneumonia and bronchitis are reported each year among infants up to the age of eighteen months due to secondhand cigarette smoke.

Parental cigarette smoke that is passed down to children increases the risk of central ear problems, wheezing and hacking and worsens asthma symptoms.

A minor who has two smoking guardians is more than twice as likely to smoke than a young person whose guardians are two nonsmokers. Young individuals are also likely to start smoking in families with a single smoking parent.

Pregnant women are likely to give birth to children whose weights are too low for their health. About 4,000 more babies would not die of pregnancy-related causes if all women stopped smoking.

About to give up

Set a deadline for stopping. Try to get a friend to give up smoking alongside you.

Pay attention to when and why you smoke. Make an effort to identify the daily activities that you occasionally engage in while smoking (e.g., driving a car or consuming your morning cappuccino).

Modify your smoking habits: Store your smokes somewhere better.

Use the other hand to smoke. While smoking, don't do anything else.

Think about how you would feel if you smoked.

Smoke merely puts, in the same way as outside.

If you think you might need a smoke, wait a few minutes. Try to think of something to do in place of smoking; you may chew gum or sip water.

Purchase each pack of cigarettes separately. Change to a cigarette brand that you could live without.

The day of your termination

Give up all of your cigarettes. Put your ashtrays away.

Change your plans for the morning. Don't take a seat at the kitchen table in a similar manner, assuming you have breakfast. Keep yourself busy.

Instead of giving in to the temptation to smoke, do something different.

Suggest other items to ingest, such as a toothpick, gum, or hard candies.

At the end of the day, reward yourself for not smoking. Go watch a movie or take part in your pet's feast outside.

Staying away from

If you find yourself feeling drowsier or more agitated than usual, try not to worry; these feelings will pass.

Make an effort to exercise by going for walks or bicycle rides.

Think about the advantages of quitting, such as the amount of time you save as a nonsmoker, the health advantages for you and your loved ones, and the example you set for others. Keeping an optimistic outlook will get you through the difficult times.

If you're feeling anxious, try to stay busy, think about solutions, acknowledge that smoking could make things a little worse, and go do something else.

Eat regular dinners. It is worth noting that the desire to smoke can be mistaken for hunger.

With the money you save by not purchasing cigarettes, start a cash container.

Inform them you've given up smoking, and the majority of them will be supportive. Many of your smoking friends should be aware of your quitting strategy. Talking to people about your stopping is ideal.

Don't let it depress you if you trip and smoke. Many former smokers made multiple attempts to quit before they were finally successful. Again, stop.

The Desire to Give Up

I have met a few folks who have successfully quit using drugs or alcohol on their own. These people understood that in order to successfully stop, they needed to make a change. Not to add, their lives transformed in a way that was both financially and healthily beneficial when they gave up smoking.

One of the folks I know who gave up smoking went on to launch a chain of restaurants. Although it's not as large as McDonald's, he still owns a $600,000 home. He left his salaried position as a manager to launch a business that takes first place in the industry in which it operates.

Giving up smoking not only helps you change your perspective but also enables you to adjust your spending. You will get the most out of your time if you give up cigarettes. Cigarettes undoubtedly hold you back—a lot.

Though it might not seem like much, everything adds up.

Smoking takes three minutes if you smoke quickly. One cigarette takes an average smoker six to eight minutes to finish. You may lose more than an hour of time doing anything worthwhile or even enjoyable if you smoke even half of a pack in a single day.

Want is all that is needed. Nothing compares to giving up smoking. Knowing that you won't smell like an ashtray anymore is empowering.

Are you the kind of person who tells yourself, "I quit before, I can quit again," as a justification for continuing to smoke now and quitting later? Some folks who are in their 60s still smoke cigarettes because of that thinking. If they don't already have a significant health issue, it won't be long before they do.

Being cautious in this society is difficult. We consider ourselves unbeatable unless anything untoward occurs. What takes place if it's too late? Would you be prepared to accept that risk? Would you rather suffer later in life or live now? Would you rather live now as fully as possible or still get to live later?

For the first week after quitting smoking, you will experience cravings on a daily basis. Those cravings will be stronger on certain days than on others. You will need to be resolute and certain that giving up cigarettes is something you genuinely want for yourself in order to cope. You most likely won't if you have the smallest doubt that you can't.

If you start to doubt yourself when trying to stop smoking, you can end up buying another pack. Believing that you lack the stamina to endure for an additional hour could be your undoing.

However, did you not just abstain from smoking for one hour? It's difficult the first day, but if you can manage to go the entire day without smoking, you can handle the next day as well.

Understanding your motivation for quitting will help you muster the necessary strength. When you begin to crave or feel triggered, use this as your shoulder to lean on. A newborn child is one of the most frequent reasons I have seen people give up smoking cigarettes. That being said, this does not imply that having a child is necessary in order to stop smoking. Every rationale is equally potent as the others.

There can be more than one reason why you want to give up smoking. I wanted to stop smoking for many reasons. Emotions of being out of breath following a staircase climb. Few things are more embarrassing for a man than having difficulty lifting something over twenty pounds and managing to carry it a few yards without panting heavily at the end.

Not only would giving up smoking extend your life, but it would also result in annual cost savings of thousands of dollars. I was living paycheck to paycheck in part because of my smoking habit. With all the money I have wasted on cigarettes, I could purchase a car or maybe a house.

Completing the Procedure

Make plans for life to return to normal. It won't take long for quitting to seem normal. You will begin to revert to your regular daily routine and establish new customs and habits related to your life as a nonsmoker.

In any event, you may have briefly considered smoking "just one cigarette," especially while everything is still running smoothly. Remember that there is never just one cigarette. It's a protracted cycle of despair from which you have emerged.

Give yourself credit for the moments, such as in social situations, when you are happy to be free. Make a big investment in the fact that you have given up smoking and in yourself.

If you're experiencing problems, seek professional assistance. In the unlikely event that you're having trouble stopping on your own, you can need to hunt for additional professional assistance around your Allen Carr with booking. The obvious option, if you must discontinue using Allen Carr's method, is to get in touch with his organization via their website. They provide book readers with support for free.

Support groups are typically available at mental health facilities, where individuals who are trying to quit talking are led in conversations by a trained physician or specialist.

A non-profit organization called Opiates Anonymous hosts support meetings for recovering addicts. Through NA's website, you may locate events taking place in your area.

If you're finding it difficult to give up smoking, go to your physician. You could also seek the advice of a qualified specialist to see whether certain simple but difficult subjects are contributing to your dependency.

The request was fulfilled with loved ones' assistance.

Remember that you cannot quit smoking by yourself. As you continue your recovery, be open and honest with those closest to you about your decision to stop, and ask for their support.

Ask your family members who smoke to give up before you or to give you their cigarettes.

When you're having a craving, find out if you can think about them. Choose people who are easy to talk to and empathetic.

If someone doesn't support your decision, it's best to quickly distance yourself from them. Compulsion is fueled by pessimism.

A small initial yield

There appears to be a downward trend in US deaths from lung and oral cancer. This has led to the adoption of comparable laws and their fervent implementation in a number of States. Thirteen states have passed laws prohibiting smoking in public areas and workplaces; however, few of those states also have bars, demonstrating that progress has been made, and many of the objectives remain unmet.

Few limit it to upscale establishments like bars and restaurants. While it is illegal in all 50 states as well as the District of Columbia to sell tobacco to minors, the enforcement of these laws has been essentially nonexistent.

Approximately 70% of smokers who are actively quitting make the decision to stop, and at least 45% of them do so for a person before giving up and succumbing to the deadly grip of smoking once more. Each year, only around 2.5% of smokers are able to reach the pinnacle and put up smoking for good. Giving up smoking offers major and immediate health benefits to men and women of all ages. Smokers who give up before turning 50 have a nearly halved likelihood of dying in the next 15 years.

Hen in contrast to those who continue to smoke.

Actions were conducted by AHCPR.

A variety of activities are successful in encouraging individuals, according to the expert panel for Awareness via Mass Communication and Rectification (AHCPR), Agency for Healthcare Research and Quality.

● A therapist's straightforward advice to stop makes thirty percent of people think about giving up this bad habit under duress.

● Individual and group counseling almost doubles the likelihood of stopping.

Approximately 40% of individuals are contacted by phone hotlines and support lines.

● Nicotine replacement therapy is used to address the remaining issues. Psychotherapy and medication are provided as additional, paid services in order to treat addiction and accomplish complete quitting of smoking.

● Jobs in food, hospitality, and other service industries

Teens, who comprise 22% of the 5.5 million total workforce, are 50% more likely than the general population to pass away from lung cancer. Reducing the population's unwanted exposure to secondhand smoke can be achieved by appropriate planning, policy, process execution, and clinical and educational interventions. Strategies for public policy include stringent worksite regulations, strong clean indoor air laws, and enforcement of public health limitations. ● Campaigns for public awareness and neighborhood-based efforts to prohibit smoking in public areas have significantly decreased the amount of secondhand smoke that is exposed to by both adults and children. Take out the passive voice. Moke can only lead to a reduction in pediatric respiratory ailments and associated illnesses. It can also greatly minimize the 500,000 yearly medical visits that are ascribed to children's worsening asthma.

The American Academy of Paediatrics has, in turn, recommended medical professionals educate parents about the risks that passive smoking poses to their developing lungs and provide guidance on how to shield their kids from this potentially fatal health issue.

WORKING TECHNIQUES

Determine when to give up. Choose the day you're going to stop smoking. Mark that day on your calendar and inform your loved ones—if any—that you will be quitting on that particular day. See this day as a turning point in your life—a transition from being a smoker to a better, new nonsmoker.

Throw away every cigarette you own. Many people find it challenging to give up cigarettes because of their temptation. Thus, dispose of everything—lighters, ashtrays, and yes, even the packs you have in your emergency supply package.

Clean every article of apparel. You may eliminate the cigarette scent as much as possible by washing every article of clothing and having your sweaters and jackets dry-cleaned. You should clean your car if you smoke in it.

Think about the things that provoke you. It goes without saying that you are aware of the circumstances that make you more inclined to smoke, including just after a meal, at your closest friend's house, while drinking coffee, or when driving. Any situation when smoking feels automatic is a trigger. After you've determined what triggers you, consider the following advice:

Break the link. For a few weeks, if you smoke while driving, consider using the bus, walking, or receiving a lift to school in order to kick the habit. Try doing something different, like going for a walk or talking to a buddy, if you typically smoke after eating.

Modify the address. To avoid having to smoke in your car when eating takeaway with your friends, choose to sit at a restaurant.

Use anything other than smokes. It could be hard to get used to without having a cigarette or holding something in your hand. Stock up on lollipops, sugar-free gum, mints, toothpicks, and carrot sticks if this problem affects you.

SMOKING CIGARETTES CAUSES NEARLY ONE IN FIVE FATALITIES.

The three greatest smoking-related deaths are chronic obstructive pulmonary disease, lung cancer, and cardiovascular disease (COPD). Apart from the "top three," smoking has also been connected to diabetes, hip fractures, osteoporosis, problems getting an erection, infertility, stomach ulcers, gum disease, and a host of other ailments.

Quitting smoking can extend your life. Though giving up is best done as soon as possible, it's never too late. There are real benefits to giving up, even at 80 years old!

3: The Advantages of Living Without Smoking

Beyond only lowering the risk of smoking-related diseases, quitting smoking has several advantages. We'll look at the various ways that giving up smoking might enhance your general health and wellbeing in this chapter.

Better Health of the Respiratory System The most obvious advantage of stopping smoking is better respiratory health. Breathing becomes easier a few days after stopping as the body starts to heal damaged lung tissue. The likelihood of lung disorders such as chronic bronchitis, respiratory infections, and other conditions diminishes with time.

Improved Heart Health The biggest cause of death in the US, heart disease, has smoking as a key risk factor. Giving up smoking can help lower blood pressure as well as lower the risk of heart disease, stroke, and other heart problems. After quitting, blood circulation improves, and the risk of heart attack decreases in a matter of months.

Decreased Cancer Risk Many cancers, including those of the mouth, throat, bladder, kidney, and pancreas, are mostly brought on by smoking. Your body can start to heal some of the harm that smoking has caused by stopping, and you will have a much lower chance of getting these kinds of cancer.

Enhanced Dental Health: It is well known that smoking causes gum disease, discolored teeth, and foul breath. You can enhance your oral health and lower your chance of gum disease, which can result in tooth loss, by giving up smoking.

Enhanced Vigour and Energy Smoking can lead to exhaustion and low energy, which makes it more difficult to engage in physical activity. It's possible that giving up smoking can give you more energy and endurance, which will make it simpler for you to work out and do other physical activities.

Improved General Health Additionally, giving up smoking might enhance your general well-being and standard of living. You might have better digestion, fewer headaches, and fewer colds and respiratory infections. Furthermore, giving up smoking can lessen the chance of developing wrinkles and fine lines early in life.

Conserving Cash Ultimately, you can save a substantial sum of money by giving up smoking. Since cigarettes may get expensive very quickly, giving up smoking can save a lot of money over time.

Helping A Loved One Or Friend To Stop Smoking

It is imperative that you cannot make a friend or loved one and give up cigarettes; it must be their decision. If, on the other hand, they actually decide to give up smoking, you can support them and try to ease the pressure to give up. Examine the various available treatment options and discuss them with the smoker; just be careful not to give advice or condemnation. You can also help someone who smokes overcome their cravings by going on various activities with them and by continuing to smoke alternatives, like gum, nearby.

Don't make a friend or family member feel bad if they make a mistake or relapse. Honor the time they spent quitting smoking and encourage them to try again. Your assistance can make a big difference in helping your loved one finally kick the vice for good.

Section Four:

AFTER YOU START TO QUIT

Try all of the techniques you decide on. Try a different attack strategy if the first one doesn't work. But after two or three months, if you haven't reduced your drinking after all, you might have to give up alcohol completely, receive treatment from a professional, or do both.

Beginning Pointers

You can test out a handful of the procedures below, and at the conclusion, you can add your own. Set aside maybe two or three to work on in the next week or so.

Maintain A Document.

Keep track of how much you're drinking. Choose a method that suits you, such as keeping drinking tracker cards in your wallet (see the previous section), creating a kitchen schedule, or writing notes on a PDA or scratch pad for your phone. Keeping a journal of the drinks you have before consuming them could help you cut back when necessary.

Measure and Count.

Understand the typical drink estimations so that you can count your drinks with certainty. Measure out beverages at home. When you're not at home, it could be difficult to follow instructions, particularly when it comes to blended cocktails. You can also occasionally be receiving more alcohol than you want. Asking the host or server not to "top off" a portion of the filled glass is necessary when it comes to wine.

Plan Your Objectives.

Decide how many drinks you'll consume over the course of the next seven days, as well as how long you want to drink. It makes sense to abstain from alcohol for a few days. The consumers who exhibit the lowest rates of alcohol consumption problems tend to remain within the usually safe cutoff limits.

"Generally safe" doesn't mean "no gamble." Customers may experience problems even within these cutoff lines if they drink too rapidly, are weak, or are more experienced (those over 65 are generally advised to have no more than three drinks quickly and seven total every week).

You may need to drink less or none at all, depending on your health and what alcohol means for you.

Both distance and speed.

If you do decide to drink, settle into a consistent pace. Taste gradually. Every hour, have around one ordinary beverage made with liquor. Use "drink spacers": switch to a non-alcoholic beverage like water, soda, or juice for every other one.

Add Food.

Avoid drinking when you have an empty stomach. Eat something to let the alcohol absorb into your system more gradually.

Look for substitutes.

If drinking has taken up a lot of your time, use your free time to develop healthy new hobbies, friendships, and pastimes or to make up for ones you may have missed. If you've relied on alcohol to manage mindsets, adjust to problems, or be more acceptable in social situations, then find other excellent ways to handle those aspects of your life.

Giving Up on "Triggers."

What triggers your need to drink alcohol? If you feel that certain individuals or places force you to drink when you don't want to, try to avoid them. If certain activities, times of day, or emotions trigger the temptation to drink, schedule something else to do instead. If you think that drinking at home is a problem, store very little alcohol there.

Organize Your Urges.

When a drive strikes and you are unable to avoid a trigger, consider the following options: Remember why you are changing (you might put your reasons in a physical document or keep them in an easily accessible electronic communication).

Conversely, you could discuss the matter with a trustworthy person. Conversely, you could partake in a fit of distraction as a legitimate pastime or a non-alcoholic side hobby. Alternatively, rather than resisting the urge, accept it and let it pass without giving in, knowing that it will eventually peak like a wave and pass.

In addition, go to the parts that follow for help managing your want to drink.

Recognize Your "No."

It's likely that occasionally, you will be offered a drink even though you don't need one. Prepare a standard, persuasive "no, much obliged" response. You are more ridiculous to clasp beneath the faster you are prepared to say no to these offers. In the unlikely event that you stumble, it gives you time to think of reasons to continue. Furthermore, refer to the supplementary sections to aid in the development of your capacity for refusing drinks.

What Are The Dangerous Ingredients In Cigarettes And How Can They Affect You?

More than 7,000 compounds, many of which are poisonous and can have major negative effects on health, are found in cigarette smoke. The consequences of some of the most dangerous compounds included in cigarettes are listed below:

1 Tar: Burning tobacco produces tar, a black, sticky material. Numerous dangerous substances are included in it, such as polycyclic aromatic hydrocarbons (PAHs), which are known to cause cancer.

2 Carbon Monoxide: Burning tobacco releases carbon monoxide, an odorless, colorless gas. It lowers the body's capacity to absorb oxygen, which can

cause heart troubles and other health concerns.

3 Formaldehyde: A highly hazardous chemical, formaldehyde is a component in many goods, including cigarette smoke. It has been connected to major health issues like cancer.

4 Acetone: A colorless, flammable liquid, acetone is a solvent utilized in many different applications. It has been connected to health concerns like cancer and respiratory disorders and is also present in cigarette smoke.

5 Ammonia: Applied in numerous industrial processes, ammonia is a highly reactive chemical. It has been connected to several major health issues, including cancer and heart disease, and is also present in cigarette smoke.

6 Lead: Cigarette smoke contains lead, a heavy metal that is harmful. Lead is

present in many products. Serious health issues that may arise from it include anemia, nervous system issues, and brain damage.

7 Cadmium: Cigarette smoke, among other products, contains the hazardous heavy metal cadmium. It can result in major health issues like cancer, anemia, and damage to the kidneys.

There are a lot more dangerous substances in cigarette smoke; the list above is not all-inclusive. Quitting smoking is the best strategy to prevent smoking's harmful consequences on your health. I would advise you to speak with your doctor or look for assistance from a local support group or quitline if you're thinking about stopping. They can give you the information and resources you need to successfully quit smoking, as well as assist you in comprehending the dangers of smoking.

12: Relapse Prevention and Emotional Support

Establishing a network of friends, family, or support organizations. Techniques for staying smoke-free and avoiding relapses

Section 1: Establishing a Network of Support

1.1 The Value of Compassionate Assistance

It can be a difficult and emotional road to stop smoking. A strong support system may offer priceless accountability, empathy, and encouragement.

1.2 Family and Friends

Inform your close friends and family members that you have decided to give up smoking. Discuss your objectives, difficulties, and advancements with them. Their understanding, encouragement, and support can make a big difference in your path. They are able to encourage you in your endeavors, support you through trying times, and serve as a constant reminder of your goal to live a smoke-free life.

1.3 Assistance Teams

Participating in a support group designed specifically for people who want to stop smoking helps foster a feeling of camaraderie and common experiences. These support groups provide a secure environment for you to talk about your experiences, ask for guidance, and learn insightful things from people who are walking in your shoes. Numerous local community organizations, online support groups, and smoking cessation programs provide chances to interact with people and get continuous assistance.

Section 2: Techniques for Avoiding Relapse and Sustaining an Alcohol-Free Lifestyle

2.1 Recognizing Triggers and Creating Coping Mechanisms

Relapse prevention requires both knowing your triggers and creating strong coping mechanisms. Think back to the circumstances, feelings, or occurrences that would tempt you to smoke once more. Make a strategy to deal with these triggers, including doing deep breathing exercises, contacting your support system, or engrossing yourself in a diverting activity. You may prevent relapses and continue living a smoke-free life by proactively addressing triggers and putting in place coping mechanisms.

2.2 Stress Reduction Methods

One of the main causes of smoking relapses is stress. It is essential to learn good coping mechanisms if you want to stay smoke-free. Investigate techniques for reducing stress, such as yoga, meditation, exercise, and journaling. T

2.3 Nutritious Ways of Living

Maintaining a smoke-free life can be facilitated by using healthy lifestyle practices. Prioritize engaging in activities that enhance general well-being, such as consistent exercise, enough sleep, and a balanced diet. Physical activity improves mood, lowers stress levels, and helps you avoid gaining weight—something that some people worry about after they stop smoking. Making self-care a priority and leading a healthy lifestyle can help you succeed in the long run.

2.4 Reflection and Mindfulness

Practicing mindfulness and introspection can help you become more self-aware and maintain your commitment to your quitting goals. Think back on your path, rejoice in your successes, and recognize your advancements.

Relapse prevention techniques and emotional support are essential for a successful quit attempt. Furthermore, relapse prevention techniques like trigger identification, coping mechanism development, stress management, healthy lifestyle adoption, and mindfulness training will support you in keeping your smoke-free existence. Recall that asking for help is a show of strength and that you are not traveling this path alone. We will provide you with parting words, inspiration, and direction as you embrace your smoke-free future in the last of this ebook.

The positive aspect

A combined anti-tobacco campaign and higher tobacco product taxes have resulted in a sharp decline in the number of smokers.

Massachusetts and California had lower rates of cigarette smokers than other US states.

The Minnesota Heart Health Program observed a forty percent decrease in the number of community smokers at various formal events. The primary objective of this quit-smoking program was also a combined school-based curriculum. A preliminary assessment from the American Stop Smoking Intervention Study (ASSIST) later revealed a 7% decrease in the number of smokers in each of the 17 ASSIST States. Cigarette advertising and promotions should be banned in order to make tobacco products less alluring to youth.

Additionally, pro-tobacco messaging should be vigorously rebutted in order to quickly and effectively reach sizable segments of the population.

The most successful ways to stop tobacco usage are, by far, those that involve television, radio, and other mass media.

Radio, magazines, and other media are used to reach broad, targeted audiences with information and educational messages; to boost public support for tobacco control policies and programs; to reinforce social norms that encourage abstinence from tobacco use; and to counteract the pro-use messaging and imagery of tobacco marketing and public relations campaigns.

Reducing the attraction of smoking

Reversing the current societal tendency that condones tobacco use is necessary to lessen the appeal of tobacco to youth. To bring about this change, we must oppose the billion-dollar cigarette promotion and advertising campaigns that mislead young, sensitive brains about tobacco use. Counter-advertising campaigns have been funded by Arizona, California, and Massachusetts in an attempt to remove such exaggerated tobacco usage appeals and draw attention to the existing risks.

Enclosed in the sheath of a puff inhaled. They were successful in informing young people about the harmful effects of tobacco use on their appearance, performance, and health. Preliminary data indicates that the media efforts have reached the youth, adults, and multicultural populations in those States, and they have been successful in achieving their objectives.

Over the past few years, advances in technology have accepted that there is no such thing as a "safe cigarette." Reducing the nicotine and tar content of tobacco products, as well as adjusting the proportions of tobacco-specific compounds and nitrosamines used in other tobacco products, are among the issues that have been brought up and debated.

Cigarette prices increase in response to decreases in cigarette demand. The rate of smoking and chewing tobacco among adults and children increases when the excise charge on tobacco goods is increased.

For every 10% increase in cigarette prices, adult smoking rates decrease drastically by 4%.

Because teen smoking rates are more sensitive to price, there is a 7.6–12%

decrease in smoking rates for every 10% increase in cigarette pricing.

Monitor your smoking habits.

You'll be in a better position to stop smoking and have a smoke-free life if you are aware of and monitor your smoking habits.

What habits do smokers have?

The frequency, timing, and conditions around your smoking habit are referred to as your smoking patterns. In order to stop smoking and prevent relapse, it is essential to comprehend these patterns.

Determine triggers

You can learn more about the situations, feelings, and routines that make you want to smoke by keeping track of your smoking patterns.

Track developments

As you attempt to stop smoking, keeping a record of your smoking habits might help you track your success.

Assess accomplishments

You can assess what is and is not effective in your attempts to stop smoking by monitoring your smoking habits. You can use this knowledge to modify your plan of quitting and raise your chances of success.

How to monitor your smoking habits

Maintain a notebook.

One easy and efficient strategy to monitor your smoking habits is to keep a notebook of the times and reasons you smoke.

Employ a smoking app.

You may track your smoking habits and track your success as you quit using a number of smartphone apps.

Put on a gadget.

Wearable technology, like fitness trackers, can track your smoking habits by keeping an eye on your stress levels and physical activity.

Keep track of triggers.

When you smoke, write down the circumstances that got you started. Utilizing this knowledge will help you recognize and control your triggers.

Monitor your cravings

Note the times and intensity of your desires. Using this knowledge, one can decide on the most effective methods for controlling cravings and preventing relapses.

Controlling Your Smoking Habits

Make a plan to stop.

Make a quit plan that considers your triggers, urges, and habits after you've determined your smoking routines.

Look for substitutes

Determine substitute pursuits or coping techniques that will assist you in controlling your cravings and triggers.

Seek assistance

It can be difficult to stop smoking, so it's critical to have a support network in place to get you through the difficult periods. To get accountability and support, think about getting in touch with a quitting buddy or joining a support group.

Continue to move.

Engaging in physical exercise can help lower stress, control appetites, and enhance general health.

Steer clear of triggers.

At least while you're first trying to stop smoking, try to stay away from situations that make you feel like smoking.

Honor accomplishments

As you strive toward quitting, acknowledge and celebrate your victories. This might support your motivation and goal-focused focus.

One of the most important steps in stopping smoking is tracking your smoking habits. Understanding the circumstances, timing, and frequency of your smoking habit will help you quit and prevent relapse.

Remain Inspired

Over the years, many smokers have made unsuccessful attempts to stop smoking. I occasionally witness young people being pressured by their parents to give up. Adults are sometimes forced to attend seminars by doctors, and other times; they are duped into going by friends and family into thinking it would be like going out to dinner. This strategy works well most of the time.

The Authority

Nobody would certainly argue that these individuals had the will or determination to give up smoking. While some smokers may have some incentive, the majority are driven to stop. Nonetheless, knowing about nicotine addiction and its therapy can encourage individuals to give it up. The goal of seminars is to impart as much knowledge as feasible.

It's critical to comprehend the causes of smoking, the best ways to quit, and how to maintain one's freedom. It's critical for anyone thinking about giving up to comprehend these four areas. Smokers who are not well-versed in these areas will find it difficult to give up.

In order to assist a smoker in realizing that the myths and emotions around smoking are false, it is essential to comprehend the reasons behind their smoking.

The majority of smokers think they smoke because they want to, but in reality, they smoke because they have no other choice. Their bodies demand that they smoke because they are addicted to nicotine. They are dependent on drugs. This is the vital first action.

As with other 12-step programs and addiction, it's critical to acknowledge your helplessness over the drug. It's critical to understand that, despite your belief that smoking would help you unwind, it was actually making you more stressed out or, more precisely, it was changing how you responded to tension. Smoking actually depletes your energy, despite your belief that it is healthy. Many smokers think that smoking makes it simpler to enjoy yourself and have an active social life. On the other hand, it may really make it harder for you to meet new people and engage in a variety of activities.

Not only does it make you more energetic and lively, but it also makes you engage in a lot of antisocial activity. You refused to attend gatherings where smoking was prohibited and smoked in public areas. It is easy to understand why someone ought to give up smoking.

The issue is that most people are unaware of how dangerous it is. Many people have a sense of helplessness when fully realizing the risks associated with smoking. Over time, it's critical to understand that giving up smoking is a battle for survival. This knowledge is essential for managing sporadic thoughts that an ex-smoker may experience due to situations and events in their lifetime.

The following advice may come as a shock to most people: When people discover smoking is killing them, they first give it up. Most of these individuals gave up smoking abruptly. Saying, "don't let an error bring you back smoking," will help you avoid getting off. This holds equal weight as advising an alcoholic in recovery, "don't let any drink make you go back to drinking," or a heroin addict, "don't let a little shot make you go back to using." Don't allow a mistake to cause you to resume smoking. "Do not err!" should be the takeaway.

A blunder can be defined as an error, a random occurrence, a slip, a puff, or just one. This is the main thing that will make quitting challenging. If you overlook this idea, or worse, if you don't recognize it at all, failure is nearly a given.

Education has proven to be an effective strategy for smoking cessation. I've seen that a thousand times. This is not just a matter of warning smokers about the risks associated with smoking. This aids in the smoker's comprehension of the negative effects smoking has on one's appearance, mental health, and finances. Thousands of ex-smokers have found that my own understanding is a useful tool for maintaining their resolve to stop smoking. As long as they remember the reasons behind their initial decision to stop smoking, they will remain resolute.

Is it possible to motivate a smoker to quit? Long-term smokers who smoke cigarettes are often driven individuals. It's likely that anyone who visits a quit smoking clinic or types "quit smoking" into an Internet search engine has some initial concerns and wants more information on how to quit, even though not all smokers are motivated.

Basically, "yes" when asked if someone is motivated to stop smoking. A motive drives most smokers.

You can't give up smoking without giving up cigarettes. Your life will be saved by this.

www.ingramcontent.com/pod-product-compliance
Lightning Source LLC
Chambersburg PA
CBHW052148110526
44591CB00012B/1891